Visibility at Zero

Visibility at Zero

Poems

Austin Kodra

4/14/16
(Carbondale, IL

Kirk,
My eternal gratitude for everything you've done to put this all together. Your enthusiasm is so genuine. I hope you find something in these pages that resonates.

Iris Press
Oak Ridge, Tennessee

Design by Robert B. Cumming, Jr.

Library of Congress Cataloging-in-Publication Data

Names: Kodra, Austin, 1989-
Title: Visibility at zero : poems / Austin Kodra.
Description: Oak Ridge, Tennessee : Iris Press, [2015]
Identifiers: LCCN 2015037568 | ISBN 9781604542363 (pbk. : alk. paper)
Classification: LCC PS3611.O3616 A6 2015 | DDC 811/.6—dc23 LC record available at http://lccn.loc.gov/2015037568

Acknowledgments

My sincerest thanks to the editors and staffs of these publications for first acknowledging the following poems (occasionally in slightly different forms) in this manuscript:

The Adroit Journal: "Hiding in the Birds"
Animal: A Beast of a Literary Magazine: "Distance from the Slaughterhouse"
Barnstorm: "Against Nostalgia"
Concho River Review: "U.S. History, 11th Grade"
Connotation Press: An Online Artifact: "Concussed" and "Woman Killed after Crashing Stolen Cop Car"
Harpur Palate: "Cello, 8th Grade"
Mason's Road: "Visibility at Zero"
Prime Number Magazine: "Parentless, in Our Childhood Homes"
Sling Magazine: "Attempts at Transcribing My Grandfather's Death by Emphysema"
Still: The Journal: "Breakdown, Bakertown Road," "Driving I-24 through Kentucky at night, I think how easy it would be," and "Engagement Picture by a Barn"
Superstition Review: "In What Could Only Be Suffering" and "Passing Out"

Many thanks to the following people, who have been instrumental in making what once seemed wishful thinking a reality. This book is as much yours as it is mine: Cathy Kodra, Judy Jordan, Josh Bontrager, Allison Joseph, Jon Tribble, Ruth Awad, Rodney Jones, Josh Robbins, Marilyn Kallet, Art Smith, Staci Schoenfeld, Zach Macholz, M. Brett Gaffney, Maggie Graber, and many more than I can count.

Also thanks to the Department of English at Southern Illinois University Carbondale for gifting me time to write and an opportunity to teach.

Table of Contents

I

II

III

I

In What Could Only Be Suffering

From front porches, the other mothers and fathers
have called their sons and daughters inside
from the churning blue machinery
of night wheeling into place.

Where is the last boy left outside to go now,
abandoned in the honeyed buzz of street lamps?

All these summer dusks the same,
and until tonight he hasn't wandered,
only slouched with legs sprawled in a dirt patch
in the park and scrawled his kingdom
from scratch with a twig until it was too dark
to see: Canopied forest, copper filigree,
monkeys carving laws into soft bark—
dusted clean each day by bike wheels or shoes.

To the other mothers and fathers
who must know his name
is not the echo of any call,
this absence must seem lonely, tragic.
Over pork chops they imagine
what happened in his home,
discuss it in bed before hitting the lights.

So what makes the boy decide,
on this night—instead of building something
to be brushed away—to follow darkness
to the neighborhood creek
where not tonight but some nights
the older boys sneak swigs of clear liquor
and slur about girls they believe to be women?

Why, when he finds on a muddy bank
a bullfrog moaning open and shut
the bag of its throat, does he spring free
the pen knife he stole from his father's fishbowl
of wishing pennies, its blade snagging a gleam
of moonlight off the still water?

Why, if not hungry or threatened
or playing to a pack of leaders,
does he cloak himself in the blue-black,
scoop the slippery mass in his fist,
grip its back legs, and skim the sharpened edge
across each inch of skin as the damp body
writhes in what could only be suffering?

If the other mothers and fathers saw,
they'd say the boy has a rage that's silent
and spreading like lichen up a tree.
They'd shake their heads,
wonder who'd been drunk or negligent
and fear their own to be next.

But the truth is nobody sees.
Nobody witnesses the care,
the precision, the fine slit across the neck,
the pleasure of deepening a fissure in flesh
like locking puzzle pieces.

Nobody is there when the chorus
of his forest kingdom dies,
when he drops the lump
that used to be frog, leaves it to rot,
its warm blood black and begging
from the near-invisible wound he's made.

Woman Killed after Crashing Stolen Cop Car

Interstate 75, Bradley County, TN

We are so close to the convergence
of what is sacred and what has collapsed.

At mile marker 22, in the median,
in the gap between tongues of asphalt,
two boys howl for their mother
from the dark muscle of their lungs.

We brake to a crawl but do not stop.
The boys wade waist deep in grass
that hooks like question marks at the tips.
Mouths hinged wide, the boys are birds
that cannot yet feed themselves.

We do not know then that they
have just watched their mother
stab an officer, wave a knife like a wand,
and disappear in his car, shots ringing,
popping against the metal body
as she speeds off, as she makes her choice.

We are here, in this moment
of such great suffering.
We almost reach from our windows.
We almost touch their faces.

Imaginary Friend

Truman lives out of a suitcase in a motel.
He holds dearly some distant joy
in firing up that grand machine
that spits ice into a bucket,
in not cleaning up after himself.

Each night he pulls and pulls outfits
like a magician's scarves from his luggage,
stares into a scratched mirror above the sink,
and calls himself *asshole* again and again
because that's how I left him.

When we were young together,
Truman listened. Because he has no dreams
I hadn't once plucked from the stars,
he lists the ones he can recall:

3rd grade spelling teacher,
a chef without a cookbook,
35 and living with his parents—

He chews his fingernails down to nubs,
tries with no good fortune to break the old habits.
He circles both a track into the rug
and the question of how to begin again,
and on the flat tube TV filmed with dust,
Truman watches marathons of *Press Your Luck*.

And when those strange faces stop
their spinning light on big-bucks-no-whammies,
when their eyes gleam with something
Truman remembers but cannot name,
he nudges aside the lone window's curtain
and squints hard to see as far as he can into the night.

Distance from the Slaughterhouse

We lived somewhere deep in the scorch—
only town for miles sprung from cracked clay,
split by a two-lane capillary,
a dried-blood highway leading
in from the desert, out to the desert.

Each Thursday for four years we ate
at the roadhouse edged with needled bushes
and rock gardens. *Like Friday but without the crowd,*
my father would say, and we'd stick to our shadows
at a corner table under mosaic light.

Each week, he ordered baby-back ribs
laid out in a glistening arch
beside mashed potatoes and coleslaw.

He stuffed the bib with a cartoon pig
down his collar, called for extra sauce.
Sucked meat off the bones
like he was playing a harmonica.

Leaned back, whistled, joked—
Should have worn a looser pair of pants.

We were close and happy and never thought
about the distance from what held us
together, the distance from the skinned and bled
slabs hanging slack from hooks, like winter coats.

Instead we'd ride home silent,
cradling the lions of our stomachs.
I'd press my face to the glass,
not knowing then that somewhere far away
the moon was a bolt stunner
or a curved blade bleeding light from black.

Spring Ball, San Angelo, TX

At ball fields built over cleared brush
and thatch, next to the airport
departing to no more than five destinations,
fathers in loosened ties latch
their fingers to chain link, watch the boys,
their own dreams coiled in the aluminum bats,
snagged in the leather webs.

Their thinning hair sprouts in gusts
against yellow clouds that shiver.

Standing atop the tallest bleachers,
one hollers above the thunder—
Let 'em play; a little storm ain't never hurt nobody!

I'd like not to think of them or other desires
I worry are spent—kids riding flat-tire bikes
near Rio Vista Park, a woman tucked into a hospice bed,
clasping her pastor's hands like fine china.

I'd rather imagine the boys starting up again.
Long toss and pepper. Loosing their shoulders
on shrunken diamonds. Unburdened by bad hops
off desert clover. I'd rather imagine
that this spring, in West Texas, the boys take leads
off first base in measured, sideways strides
that seem more suited for survival.

That, therefore, they'll grow in increments.
That the fathers, having lost what grace the spring
once gave them, will release the bendable bodies
that so miraculously resemble their own.

Flame and Sometimes Water

Each morning, in front of the mirror,
the mother braids her daughter's hair.
Plaits knotted loosely mean last night
was creek over stone, nothing broken,

but mostly the mother tugs the braids taut
like peach pits. Without warning, this morning,
the daughter's womb floods with the dead—

Romans laying roads that lead into but never through,
passages for the transport of olives, slaves—
She shakes and asks why she bleeds this way.

It is what we bring with us, the mother replies,
like those before carried two, and carried two across broad plains,
buffalo pelts over fractured shoulders, cupped palms bearing flame
and sometimes water. Or maybe that's what she says

in a dream, in a different life, and she instead whispers,
Don't tell your father, pulls the girl by the wrist
into the bathroom and shows her how to stop it.

The Cash Cube, 6th Grade Fundraiser

Always our parents have told us
beware of strange men offering candy—
but here's one in a polo shirt tucked into track pants
toting a rucksack of surprises,

and from simplifying fractions
we are called to the gym
to be his audience.

We know there is a catch
to free chocolate, even this young—

But don't eat 'em! Take 'em next door.
Take 'em to church. Have Pops sell 'em
to his coworkers, or Mom to the neighbors.

Pacing with the strange energy of someone
who hasn't slept in days, he pulls from the sack
and fist-pumps the possible prizes:

Who out there loves homework?
Didn't think so!
Two boxes'll get you a free pass
from Science or English or Math.

Six for movie tickets. Ten for a lava lamp.
Fifteen for a mini-gumball machine.

We'll start small—two doors down,
up the block—ring a doorbell,
knock a knocker while Dad
keeps the car running and hot.

We'll burrow our shame
in the tall necks of winter coats.

Two bucks a bar, the same we've seen
at the grocery store for one.
Most of us will shuffle back
to the car and ask to go home.

But for now the man in track pants
makes one last pitch—empty sack,
sweat dripping from his chin
like he's run wind sprints—

one last pitch for the suckers
who'll lug fifteen hundred dollars' worth,
seven hundred fifty candy bars
in countless loops around the neighborhood,
skip soccer practice, sacrifice sleepovers,
abandon ball games in the park.

And if you sell an amazing total of fifty boxes . . .
Well, bring out The Cash Cube!

Shaped like an old phone booth
with mirrored bulbs blinking its edges,
The Cube is rolled out to center court.

He steps inside, pushes a big red button,
and a flurry of cash swarms his body
like horseflies on dead meat.

His hands open then close
like a half-formed language,
like strobe lights—
these thirty seconds a vision
of what we could fall into,
open-armed, baring teeth.

We sit in awe of his waving hands,
frantic, scraping down all they can carry—
a mess of crumpled money,
a month's water bill at most,
held high like a trophy.

Advice for My Grandfather's Blessing

The sweeter the pie, the shorter the prayer.
—*Rodney Jones*

For the bland—baked chicken breast over a bed
of rice and no gravy—bless the grandchildren,
the length of summer days in remembrance of field work,
the fowl's mysterious faculties. Bless the oak table's
ancestry, yesterday's good news at the doctor,
the dog rope-tied in the cellar stairwell,
her muzzle nuzzling a constellation of shoes.

For the wife's fine applesauce and baked bread
instead of rice, bless more simply our health
and omit the chicken, for a lack of understanding
its own plight is why it is ours to eat.

For a juicier flesh—rare beef, perhaps—elide the dog
who needn't hear there is red meat to be had,
and no reason to speak of fieldwork a lifetime passed.

For something that teases the white tablecloth
from its closet shelf—bison cutlets and mashed
sweet potatoes with mushroom gravy—forget the oak table,
for it is hidden and no one will think twice about its age.

And Grandpa, for the bacon-wrapped venison tenderloin
with chanterelles in brown butter, for the blueberry crumble
with hand-whipped cream, after the long wait
between lunch and supper, with your stomach rumbling
and hands twitching for a pinch of nicotine,
no longer bless the grandchildren,
as they will not taste the difference between this
and the chicken, as they will consider the meal
merely a chore before playing the night away
while you watch and breathe oxygen from a tank.

So chop it down: *Our Father we thank You for this food and all our many blessings. Amen.*

West Texas Thunderstorm

Where grass is candle wax burning
green-wick flame; where sky is deep
bruise, amethyst and yellow; where darks
are forgotten, dry, pinned to the clothesline,
taut in wind like they're trying to remember skin;
where whistles bouncing off the spout
of a brown bottle mimic the breeze
that threads summer oak sleeves;
where bluebonnets beyond the back fence
part like mouths hinging open
for a final hymn; where chains
lifting up the wooden porch swing
twist and scrape; where the storm flinches
before it begins—faith is not found or lost.

Hail of acorns thudding a tin roof.
One fat raindrop, then another,
then a downpour blown slantwise,
then stopped.

I am eight. All of this—given.
My mother knits, and we rock heel-to-toe,
and her hands weave without her eyes
as though she's turning pages of a book
she doesn't care to read.

Our faces made skeletal in a flash of light.
Our voices swallowed in a clap of thunder.

Locked Out

Upstate New York

My mother's tee shirt is a shroud against the winter wind.
Buzz of a short-fuse porch light, gray clouds
bruised black and purple.
                           Her second husband, the man
she married before my father, clicks the lock,
pulls the drapes like a sheet over a stiff body.

★

When I ask her now, she says it could have been anything:
a jagged slice of tomato, creases folded

into a button-down, a corkscrew buried
too deeply in a drawer. *Your sister wasn't there,*

at least. She was with your grandparents. She fumbles
with a napkin ring as though she cannot

find a way to fill the hole with something lasting,
something that won't slide right back out.

★

Snow sifts into her tennis-shoe tracks, cascades
        down into cracks between the torn fabric
and her anklebones. Every few steps she peers back,
        squints toward the house hunched at night's dead end,
moonlight speckling snow drifts with a map
        of broken eggshell. A black collar of pines in the distance.
With each glance, the porch light flickers smaller.

★

I hiked the quarter mile down to the babysitter's house and stood far enough into the night that I might have been another doe frozen to her spot. I remember how he used to look at me when I'd pick up your sister. He'd ask "Everything okay up there?" Narrowed eyes, pursed lips, head tilted to the right. He was kind as far as I recall, but I was something else, a shameful beast, how I'd stayed and kept your sister there. I was twenty-three. I couldn't admit my husband was the drunken shadow of my father. Same age, same rage. That I had somehow done worse in marriage number two. That I was a doe frozen to her spot.

★

Clouds pinch another flurry
as she finds each gouged print
in the snow that led her
to the small house
at the bottom of the hill,
on the back road's edge,
and one by one she climbs
her way home, determined
to make a lone set of tracks.
She thinks, *This is how
I would erase my path,*
and she wishes for a moment
that she had no choice but to escape.

When she finally reaches home,
when the blurred chalk line of his van
gives way to its rusted-out body,
when she sees the cloak of snow
blanketing raised beds, two hours
have passed. The porch light whispers
its warning. Her husband slinks

through the door, tosses a thin blanket
over her shoulders, guides her up the icy steps.
She is more than skin-chilled,
more than numbed at the far reaches
of her fingertips and thumbs.
She follows him inside, where his hands
will warm her body, where his hands
will swaddle her in sleep.

Sunday Afternoon, Dairy Queen, Benton, IL

As the girl at the register
takes orders with a finger
looped in her hair, jaw slack
like a dog-eared book,

I'm thinking of my grandfather again.
His ventilator humming
from the kitchen like the sputtered whirr
of the soft serve machine,
like the gasp and heave at the stoplight
outside as a semi leaves town,
heads someplace else.

I'm remembering how, as a child,
when I'd visit, we'd spend
the time after breakfast
rocking on porch chairs,
guessing the colors of cars
heard from half a mile away,
waiting for lunch.

Here, muraled walls show us
how we might imagine our dinners:
burgers roaming open pasture,
fries coddled in tissue paper,
a blue sky dropping Oreos
like dirty snow.

At the front of the line,
there's an old couple—
the man in hunter's plaid,
wife happy on his arm
as though some things
never did change.

They shuffle to the counter,
mumble to each other,
debating a dipped cone
or candy chunks swirled in vanilla,
as though love had always
come down to slivers of flavor,
as though the girl levering
mounds on mounds of ice cream
would find her own sweetness.

I've forgotten that a lifetime
can pass in such a small place,
that our decisions whittle down
to the ghosts of old desires,

like my grandfather—wife
of fifty years dead, big game
rifle dusty on its rack,
black lungs rattling
like tin cups raked along bars
of prison cells he guarded—
asking himself if he might
spark one final cigarette,
muster the breath to scramble
eggs with cracked pepper
for breakfast, if he might
find one last way,
in what time is left,
to treat himself.

My Grandmother's 37th Wedding Anniversary

Anton, her husband, smokes another cigarette—
hand-rolled, a change he's made to trick himself
into believing he's saving money, saving
for a future long since come and gone.

My father holds his new bride's hand under the tablecloth.
Feet rubbing calves, knees brushing, the ways
they've already learned to hide their pleasure.

To have them all here means everything to Antonia,
who slices a cream pie that came shrink-wrapped
in foil folded like an accordion.

She plans later—while she washes her face
and Anton lies in bed blowing smoke,
staring at the ceiling as though he were looking
past a bird on a leafless branch—
to say, *He seems happy; they seem happy.*

For now, she asks who'd like coffee.
They all nod, but nobody's saying much.

Less than one year against thirty-seven
seems like the chances of spotting a blue owl
perched in a moonless winter night. Sad then,
what plans come to. Anton spills the coffee
on his leg and clutches his chest, turns purple
from the neck up, drops to the floor.

The heart's final speech, loud and erratic
and nothing about love, nothing about four decades
of relative joy. Just the panic in its voice
as it ruminates about end times. For all Anton can know,
his son doesn't grow to resent his new bride,

and they don't divorce after fourteen years.
For all he can know, his wife keeps slicing pie,
brewing coffee, stirring in one cream, two sugars.

Against Nostalgia

When my older brother was young enough
to believe in flight, he leapt from a tree
in our front yard, certain he would dip low

then swell over the sea of cornfields
beyond our fence line. The superhero cape
our mother sewed draped down his back,

his arms plunged through the scrape of branches.
Afraid he was unworthy after the failed attempt,
he wrapped himself in blankets to hide
the red lines scrawled across his body.
Never satisfied with history, he wrote
a novel at nine, trashed it at ten.

And though my memories of him this young
are borrowed, I can say it all changed
after his first girlfriend died in the passenger seat
while a drunk driver swerved into a guardrail,
and because there was no last-ditch swoop
to save her, no plot twist, no heroics,
he gave up hope such things existed—
but maybe he was just a boy fast-tracked
to manhood, learning too early what love
and death can mean, those sorrows
that anchor us from the beginning.

Which is why, now, at a bar in Boston,
divorced, happy drunk and with a job,
he tells me he doesn't like nostalgia,
the longing to step back, to recall
the fluttering cape, the longing for takeoff,
the soar over stalks razed to stubble. The drop.

Parentless, in Our Childhood Homes

During the night after my grandfather's funeral,
the night my brother and I threw a party
in our mother's house, I had the slurred thought
that somewhere beneath the layered, filmy stick
of beer spilled from tall boys, deep down,
under crumpled fast food wrappers
damp with grease and cigarette butts on beds of ash,
the coffee table still had the shine my mother
always guaranteed—magazines straightened,
smudges erased—but it wasn't until just now,
seconds ago, rain ticking shingles and car hoods,
slicking this small town's unlined streets,
on no specific occasion, years removed
from what remains of that night's memory,
that I wondered how my mother decided to fill
those same hours, both of us parentless,
in our childhood homes, and somehow my first thought
was that, for even that night, she was a mother,
that she organized her dead father's clothes into piles,
reknotted his necktie, pulled family photos
from his dresser so she wouldn't have to look
in the glare of that old life as she scrubbed
the surface until the scuffed oak lay bare.

Praise Song Against Praise Songs

Praise birdsong that halts outside your window
    and lets you sleep an extra half hour.

Praise the lyrics of your favorite tune by not belting them
    through the pitiful water dribbled from the shower.

Praise Greek myth by not spraying it like buckshot
    across an acre of your infinite prairie of dreams.

Praise this nameless *you* for skittering out the side gate
    and leaving no trace in the cul-de-sac of the mind.

Praise the old metaphor for a bad father by looking
    past the black feathers, by finding a new animal.

Or maybe, praise the understanding that praise
    cannot be siphoned, so easily put to music,

that praise is overkill for the blooming flower,
    that there is not a word in our language
        for a parent whose child is reduced to ash.

Engagement Picture by a Barn

We lucked upon this abandoned spot
on a country drive—to get away, we agreed.

Having grown behind stone and timber
and the gentle hum of a Kenmore unit,
we wanted to return to wheat that,
if we trace far enough back, delivered us here.

But crabgrass stalking the weed-eaten doorway
scratches our bare ankles. Barn swallows sputter
and shit from rotting beams. Bottle flies orbit
the musty years of mold inside.

Soon enough, night removes its gloves
to bludgeon the sky. No streetlight
to cradle us from falling into it.

Time to go, we agree, vowing to remember
with desire each warped slat and rusted nail,
as though we could tell this story at parties,
as though we could catch the dead passing through:

cows that dribbled milk, farmers and their children
who dug holes for something buried deep,
for something we couldn't even guess.
Who struck the dirt with blades like anchors.

What I learn with a girl from the Baptist church who says she'll date me if I accept Jesus Christ as my personal savior

That God is everywhere, even perched in the nest-infested belfry, tolling, alive as ever.

★

That He is the everlasting miracle, the everlasting grace for this old mountain town where everyone once knew everyone but now at night the streets empty and porch doors whine shut.

★

That—as Pastor Ron testifies into a wireless headset—the famines in Amos were famines of faith. That hunger is what makes us raise our hands to the sky to pray that bullets will one day rain down and miss us.

★

That two Sundays ago, a freshly blessed man eating at the new McDonald's across the street from the church swore on his granddaddy's grave he'd seen Lord Jesus Himself ironed into a McGriddle.

★

That when the girl tells me this headline as we idle at the drive-thru, she believes it like I believe in the places our bodies have yet to go.

★

That when I start to tell a joke and she stops me and says, *There's so much more God can offer,* she's stolen the words right off my tongue.

★

That the rain of the end-times will be long and sloppy and bald tires will skate the roller rink of asphalt, and we'll be stuck and have to pull into a parking space and the downpour will silence us both, and as the water rises sheets of rain will descend on the hood like they've been sprayed from an assault rifle God finally found the grace to take down from His rack.

The beautiful woman at the buffet says,

as clear as glass panes housing heat lamps
humming their damnedest to keep
creamed corn and hushpuppies alive,
Love is the one and only ticket—
Then comes the wash . . . wash . . . wash—
and sooner than I can suggest
scrapings from the bottom
of the popcorn shrimp, she is lost
in a steamed swamp of collard greens,
a whipped cloud of potatoes.

I sit back down at my booth
with dunes of starch and flesh
and open wide, hoping for the wash
that cascades like dirt from a spade,
the wash where all the floating pieces lock—
muck of Julys, lovers
buried in sand, field lights
built fencepost-to-post—the wash
brewed to scrub this imagined woman
who whispers mystery only I can hear.

But I can't make the switch
from tequila flask to meat and—blessed be—
my prayers are no more
than snippets of God's underwear.

All that remains: a squeaky-wheeled Oreck
sucking crumbs and dust,
a stoned kid slit-eye-soldiering
his beaten path to aluminum pans,
dumping battered chicken
on battered chicken.

Visibility at Zero

*"Two chain-reaction collisions in dense fog on a highway in southeastern
Tennessee killed 15 people today and injured more than 50."*
—New York Times, *Wednesday, December 12, 1990*

This morning, even the keyholes between weedy stalks
bulge with cotton.
                    The riven vein of interstate and exit
clots with vapor pumped from the nearby pulp mill,

and those sunk and drowning in the sea of it startle,
their faces swirling like steaming cups of coffee.

Engine blasts.
        Rigs capsized.
            Glass jigsawed
like the body splitting open.
                    They are curled in ditches,
strapped to downturned seats, hurled through windshields.

They reach for children
who sit in desks at school,
                    pad across
melting asphalt like it's a pitch-black ballroom
scattered with loaded rat traps.

Almost touching.
            They pray for rope ladders to the sky.

And like them, there are more and more who hurtle past
hollow grain silos and billboards dredging this slipstream
of highway for penance, more who count the green markers
ticking each mile like minutes, more who never

have a chance to see where a fog like this begins
and where it ends, as out of the thin, sudden air,
appears a shipwreck of gnarled metal, an ocean on fire.

II

Void

On May 26, 2002, the captain of the tugboat Robert Y. Love *accidentally crashed his barge into an I-40 bridge support in Webbers Falls, Oklahoma. A 503-foot section of the bridge fell into the Arkansas River. According to witnesses, highway traffic continued to drive into the void in the bridge created by the collapsed spans. Fourteen people died.*

"I got mad because (the Highway Patrol Officer) wouldn't let his divers go in the water, he wouldn't do anything. I got mad. I put on a set of fatigues."
—*William James Clark*

I.
William James Clark pulls over
at a rest area six miles from the bridge

Trust me.
    Something bad's happening.
       I've felt this before.

It isn't here but close.
          Like a black cloud's gonna rumble up and drop knives.

      In the parking lot, there's these two kids
      buckled in the backseat of this old, dying
      bucket. I see it in the girl's eyes—I know that look.
      She'd kill the boy this second if she could.

And in the bathroom, they've built
cameras into the stalls. Always watching.

      Look, I was born into an Army family.
    It's instinct. It's in my blood.

    Crisis rears its ugly head,
and I become
            the man I'm meant to be.

II.
The captain wakes after passing out
in the tugboat's wheelhouse and tries to remember

Say my body unconscious
and wedged upright
in the captain's chair
is a bent wind vane.

Say the drift and collision is a dream
where the lights won't turn on
and the split pier collapsing the bridge
into the river is a new day's parted hair.

Say the eleven cars and trucks
driving off the edge of the world
are pinballs dropping
toward stuck flippers.

Say the shirring water
is a shattered window.

Say it's anything but what it is,
that I can sift my hands
through the shards and touch
what—I pray—still stirs beneath.

III.
A Highway Patrol Officer speaks
to volunteers on the scene

They're itching for the green light to dive in.
I tell 'em there's nothing more they can do,
that they should all go home or follow the detour around.

Rain pounds the sound of my voice into the pavement.
An overweight man hollers from the back of the small crowd,
and all I make out is he's bitching.
Some lone guy with something to prove.
Can't see him or anyone else too well,
so no need to shout into a wall of fog.

For some reason, though, I can't shake the thought
that he's following me. I glance over my shoulder,
but there's only the downpour and a fine white mist
like a sheet my boy might wear for Halloween.

IV.

A fisherman watches from his boat

The river's murky, swollen and yellow like a bruise.
We'd set out early for a bass tournament, our lures cast
in the same arcs as those vehicles, their wheels spinning.
I fired a red flare, and two others sped to the scene,
pulled three survivors from their sinking cars.

Now they've cleared us out. Too dangerous, a current
running this fast. Doesn't seem right. A crane rakes
a dredging bucket along the riverbed for wreckage.
Heavy tackle. The rain is steady. I keep mistaking drops
hitting the river for fingertips nudging the surface.

V.

A woman waits with her daughter in her sunken car

Urge is to set her down like in the tub.
Pull my submerged purse
from under the seat, dig out my wallet,
unfold the photos of her I'd show
in line at the UGO.

But the water's climbing,
and I have to hold her up.

I have no choice but to leave like this,
watching my baby turned animal,
wailing and thrashing against me.

I allow myself a second to close my eyes
and imagine her in the pictures:
zippered in a baby sailor outfit,
fake sunflowers buttoning overalls.
The smiles I coaxed out of her
by making her stuffed monkey dance.

The water swells to my throat.
No time for prayer.
We must move on without it.

I promise, my eyes will be open
and looking into hers
when they pull us to shore.

VI.
William changes into ROTC fatigues
and practices in the mirror of a public restroom

They'll never let him help.

They'll never let a fat-civilian-nobody
dive into the current or pull the wreckage
or come up with a plan. So this is what I gotta do.

> *I'm Captain William James Clark.*
> *10th Special Forces, Afghanistan.*
> *I'm in charge now. I'm your first*
> *and direct point of contact. All developments*
> *delivered straight to me. Are we clear?*

I've ironed out the wrinkles
from the pants and shirt.

> *The tattoo? Hell yeah. See how the snake wraps*
> *the skull, how the cheekbones bulge on my triceps?*
> *See these unit patches stitched on the sleeves?*

I've scrubbed the scuffs from my black boots.
No one can see my feet. No one can say
they don't fit Army regulation.

> *Trick is you melt the polish on*
> *with a heat gun. You pick up things*
> *along the way, I suppose. You live*
> *this life long enough, you're bound*
> *to take something away from it.*

VII.

Later that night, a National Guardsman plays pool with William in the City Hall rec room

Can't shoot worth a lick.
Each time he tries to break,
the cue tip nicks the side
of the ball and the rack stays intact.
Says there was a bar in Missouri.
Says he had his own cue,
the felt was smoother, says the fluorescents
here fool his eyes. But hell, I don't mind.
Not like I'm banking off five rails,
fixing English like those pros
in suits playing trick-shot magic.
He's just a guy trying to fit in,
trying to convince himself
there's an excuse for each scratch
and mis-hit. But when it comes
to rescue operations—believe this,
the boy knows that game through and through.
Showed up this morning out of the blue,
spoke a moment or two with local police,
then brought us in and delivered the news.
Since this morning he's talked
to NTSB, FBI, FEMA, the Pentagon,
debriefed the congressman,
shook the mayor's hand,
ran trucks and cranes
and sorted personal remains
until the rain broke
and there was nothing to do
but sit back and watch the sun set.
He's lining up the 9,
and I ask him for his story.
He tells it like he's told it

a million times.
Says he was last stationed
in Afghanistan. Says before that
he was in Uganda, 10th Special Forces,
helping Rwandans get home.
Says those were dark times,
necessary times. Another scratch.
Says he'll find his groove.
Says he needs one more rack before bed.

VIII.

The Mayor of Webbers Falls, Oklahoma, holds a press conference, May 28, 2002

Let us not forget the real Army Captain and his German Shepherd.
Let us not forget the mother driving her daughter to the Tulsa Zoo.
Let us not forget the husbands and wives, the young and old, the
    locals, the Utahans and Oregonians just passing through.

Let us celebrate the true heroes of this Memorial Day tragedy.
Let us offer praise for those they pulled alive from the water.

Let this neither be scandal nor reprehension for believing in
    goodness.
Let this be memory.

As for the assailant, the fraud, the criminal
who'd best be captured and forgotten—
he's made off in a pickup truck
he lied his way into stealing.

William James Clark is not, has not been,
and will never be in the United States Army.

He fooled us with captain bars, tattoos, a uniform.
He knew who to call, what words to say,
how to say them.

I cannot defend our trust or our belief,
except to say when there are bodies drowned
in a river, you hope fate is the only evil.

We have found him out.
Civilian. An ex-con for check fraud.

I will end with this.
Let us capture him quietly and be done.
Let us repair the bridge and leave no scar.
Let us stand at the river and bow our heads in peace.
Let us grieve.

IX.
William James Clark prepares to board
a ferry in Tobermory, Canada

Authorities arrested William James Clark in Tobermory on June 6, 2002

A man who's finished his work
needs a vacation. That's why I left.
I'd done all I could,
which wasn't nearly enough.

That man needs to go hunting,
do a little fishing.

Me, a hero? I never think
like that when disaster strikes,
but I won't refuse if folks
choose to remember me that way.

All I know is the good guy deserves a sunset,
a beer-filled cooler in a truck bed,
a rifle with a long-range scope.

The good guy should wear his camouflage
in plain sight. The good guy shouldn't need
to be anyone else other than the self-
less man you trust with your life.

III

The Man Wanted for Stealing Kids

Your father tosses the rusty lock in the trash,
sets a new deadbolt on the front door.
You ask him why. *There's a man,* he says,
big, with a hook, come from nobody's sure where,
taking kids like you at night.

You peek out the half-opened door
to the two-lane highway, cars and trucks
parting neck-high weeds in the field across
from the house. You imagine the man
out past Chazy, out off U.S. 9,
where on starless nights, it's so dark
he can't tell field grass from snakes around his ankles.

You imagine him picking the lock on a small house
grazing the edge of a cornfield, tying up
the children, and—while they wait
wondering what they did wrong—
scrambling eggs and buttering toast.

As the day slips by you forget
to be afraid. The setting sun plows
rows of husks into darkness,
and the half-moon lightens only their tips.

In the living room, your father listens
to a ballgame on the radio, and you stand
at the window, watch the quiet road
flushed by a passing car or two.

After a minute of stillness, a stir.
You feel something prick your skin,
and out of the field a blurred figure
emerges, a figure you've seen so many times,

its body left open to a sudden flood of headlights
blasting the whole scene white.

You flinch for the screech and thud
of a crash that never comes, hear instead
your father's yawn as he stands behind you
and stretches, asks why you look like
you've just seen a ghost, his face
a dusty reflection in the window.

Three Versions of Truth, Somewhere in New Mexico

The first version
is an aluminum rod
sprouted from the sand:
DANGEROUS CURVE AHEAD.

Another is desert thistle,
blister beetles clutching
a boulder's dark underbelly,
the Organ Mountains
crooked and gray
like a swollen braid
of poorly sewn stitches.

The last is not quite so clear,
not so much a matter of direction
or purpose. The last lies
somewhere between the car
and it's tread-kicked cloud
of dust and pebble,
between double yellow lines
splitting two sides
of the same grave,
between the mother's humming
and the Wayne Newton song
cracking from the radio,
between the boy crying *Wolf!*
and the father's stubble,
his swerving against
the troubled road
that never curves,
only wavers
in a mirage of heat,
in an itch they all harbor
to unhook the seams
and scatter.

Cello, 8th Grade

Like holding a telephone at your fingertips.
Our teacher turned her hand from ear to chest-level
as though she was hanging up an old desk phone—

it was how we were supposed to grip our bows,
press them to string, our hacksaws with bundles
of fine nylon teeth. But instead of carving notes
from steel, we drummed the hollow out of f-holes
and laughed when told to quiet down.

We're here to find another way to speak,
she said, showing us how to slick the bows
over sticky rosin like tongues over hard candy,
unscrew and draw out endpins like measuring tapes.
We thought to ourselves the time to speak had passed.

And when she played Bach's Prelude to Suite No. 1
on the school's old Casio cassette deck, the boy
in the last chair who'd always kept to himself,
who couldn't play scales without a rabid screech
on the bridge, said the gruff sweeps across the C-string

sounded like his father he spoke to once a week,
barking orders through a prison phone:

Clean the gutters. Change the deadbolt.
Wash the windows. Make me proud, son.

And for what felt like the first time,
we didn't know what to say or do,
we only let his last note linger in our throats
until our teacher lifted her hands
and we were forced, once more, to play.

Passing Out

When it's your turn, you stand
in the middle of the road
while the other boys
skulk behind a tree
on a neighbor's lawn.

It used to be enough
to whisk the world to a pulse
and collapse on the grass
while the sky spun away,
but now the wide road
holds you straight.

You bow to it, huff its black residue.
Deep breaths. Twenty in, twenty out.

As the countdown closes in
on zero, you have no idea this
will always be a part of you—
this need to become shadow,
this compulsion to shed your body
in a heap of water and bone.

But you've seen the other boys go,
which is all the convincing it takes.
So when the count reaches nothing,
you rise up and trap the last breath
in your chest, grip your neck
where the blood pumps

until the other boys are ghosts
swaying in tree-limbed dusk,
until the numb and night flood in,
until you are little more
than a falling curtain, a shake of salt
dissolving back into the dirt.

Sometimes I think it was an act of hope,

but then I imagine his temple nestled
against the barrel, gentle trigger-pull
like scratching a bug bite behind the ear.
In the end, the world is nothing but layers:
scrims of wax and meat, memory shorn from reams
of story, a full-length mirror on plaster on lath
on which, that night, Josh, twenty, sketched
what nested deep inside, bent in lamplight—
what bucked from his skull a charging beast.

Attempts at Transcribing My Grandfather's Death by Emphysema

~~In winter, there is no light like this.~~
~~How could he~~ He's not well enough to ~~disappear~~ storytell
~~the heavy arc~~ the ten-foot bear of his logging days
or to find a hiding spot in the back yard,
swat through a high-noon net of mosquitos.

Hospital bed: sinewed foam, blue-black.

Respirator panting, morphine drip
whispering darkness over light
like a ~~fresh bruise of~~
        wound pre-bruise.

Each dusk we return to his house: fence
of ribbed logs nudging the county highway,
~~his bed~~ yellow bedspread faded with train-track rips
and ~~the fireplace slate~~ that Scotch-Taped copy
        of Old Black Witch! cloaked in a bookcase.

★

In winter, either tin-bright day or
                        made light—no
                        in-between,
~~black holes~~   no final chance
        to start the day.

Now, summer, on his porch. Waiting. Waiting.
Full trees ~~perched like crows~~ tarring like his lungs, wheeling,
sucking down the night's hot, dirty air.

★

In winter, there is no light like this.
How could he disappear?
The heavy arc,
fresh bruise of his bed,
the fireplace slate.

★

Black holes perched like crows.

There Will Not Be Any Services

A flock of those blackbirds that die suddenly
falls from the Arkansas sky onto a field of razed corn,
drops like it hit a thick cumulus of buckshot,
snaps down, a bed sheet shaken of its wrinkles.

A truck on the side of the back road's
blown a tire. A man without a spare.
He's leaning against a bed full of lawn seed
bought for next season. A man who's halfway
between town and home, waiting for a tow,
a man who at first thinks the birds are scavenging
a colony of insects and so finds no reason
not to follow the plummet, and instead of seeing
the dive and swell like the sweep of a conductor's baton,
he hears the hum of skulls drumming half-frozen soil,
watches dust and loosed feathers plume, settle.

Now, he has nothing to do but twirl the key ring
his grown daughter had engraved and spend
an hour here stunned, thinking he doesn't know
how soon he'll die or how loud it'll be when he goes
or who'll watch, from the graveyard parking lot,
his body given back to the ground.

A shovel on top of all those forty-pound bags,
but he realizes, for the birds scattered like pepper
dashed on a slab of meat, the field must do its own work.

Meanwhile, elsewhere, on the LED sign
outside Meredith Funeral Home on a corner
in small-town Illinois, a message flashes for a woman
called Darlene Miller: *There Will Not Be Any Services—*

white hyphens marching along the sign's border
like the clunk of boots in what was meant to be a silent,
dark passing. A public notice suggesting she had been forgotten
or wanted everyone to forget. That we die alone,
even in daily flocks, need not be rehashed.

For Darlene, there isn't a headstone or a procession
of loved ones tossing fistfuls of dirt, and in the solitude
after these birds, as he listens for the tow truck's groan
in the moments before he can see it coming,
the man decides when he returns he won't mourn them
with his wife but will instead call his daughter,
ask her to come home for dinner, ask her to come home soon.

October Funeral, Age Twelve

My mother was only able,
     on the morning of my grandmother's funeral,
to step inside her parents' bedroom.
     I hovered in the doorway as she shook out
each of her mother's blouses, then walked
     from closet to bed in lockstep with the dust
as it floated through the shadows.
     She spread outfits across the quilt,
by color, picked up one garment at a time,
     smelled it, breathed the cotton into her lungs
longer than I cared to watch.

★

At the Wobbly Moose, nobody mentioned
     the early Halloween decorations:
skeleton slouched in a filled bathtub,
     spiders cobwebbed, bobbing on its surface,
bats roped to the rafters. The reception.
     Bar and grill glossed in Adirondack cedar,
pine needles brushed inside by our boots.
     Outside a great-grandchild tried to eat brown snow,
and inside a man I'd never seen
     played Sinatra's "Strangers in the Night"
on the lobby's upright piano.
     As he was greeted by a line of condolences,
Grandpa, a regular,
     ordered a bowl of tomato bisque,
which blanketed in steam
     the empty seat across his table.

★

While her ashes were spread at the family plot,
      my uncle recited an elegy, which I recall
spoke of rebirth, but Grandma's dog
      took a shit on a neighboring gravesite.
My mother's eyes met mine. We laughed so hard
      we had to bury our faces in our hands
to hide a different kind of crying.

A poem that refuses to be a Poem

Moon is the wing of starling that offers light, softly, like rain,
        iridescent across the garden where we take late tea.

My breath sweeps like crow-feathers across the nape of your neck.
        We bruise the night with our blue clothes. Not our red clothes,

our blue clothes. I recite the story my father
        told me each night before bed when I was a child, his gruff song

tendering my sleep with dreams of wheat chaff
        and rosemary. (You fall into me, listening, the whites

of your eyes a grainy feldspar.) How he saw the jacarandas
        in Santiago del Estero bloom their pulmonas lavanda,

how he espaliered fig and lemon trees through a plywood trellis,
        how each morning his hands sprouted new fingers . . .

Wait.
On second thought,
nobody falls into anyone else.
If we were drinking tea in a garden in the dark
we probably would have microwaved the tea, spilled it,
burned our hands, then stomped flat a flower bed.
Really, her eyes looked like lumpy blurs
because we were both soused on wine coolers swiped
from her parents' fridge. My breathing on her
was heavy and awkward, and she kept squirming away,
and the moon looks like a circle of bird shit
spattering my windshield. Fucking birds.
My father stutters like you wouldn't believe.
He's retired and watches C-SPAN and baseball.
He's never been anywhere more fashionable
than Disney World, and he never told me stories,

only to shut up and eat the cube steak.
He broke a couple fingers, and now they're old and crooked.
I want to kill somebody in my dreams.
We were never in love, that anonymous girl and me.
Each tree I walk by is a tree.
Whatever I think is beautiful means nothing.

Elevator Operator, Fine Arts Building, Chicago, IL

Long past the era of brass handles,
his lever remains, worn against a cupped palm,
scrubbed of its reflection, flecked
with a few lingering nicks of bronze.

Murals on eight, mazurkas on ten.
Paint-blotched khakis, white gloves
to the elbow, computer bags slung
across the shoulder. He's shuttled them all

these sixty years: through the Chicago 7,
banked lighting for night games at Wrigley,
the heat-wave summer of '95,
through that November night in Grant Park.

He's lit globe lamps and rows of numbers,
his days layered with greetings and farewells
and occasional pleasantries to fill the gaps.

As he seals the French doors,
as he lifts me an octave of floors, I wonder
if he ever holds the craft he's perfected
up to the light of all the paint and pixels,
all the symphonies and dances he glides past.

I wonder if he's considered
his religious work of the gears,
the smooth groove of machine into place,
how he rose and fell straight lines while I
and the others scattered to some purpose,
having forgotten how we arrived.

Luckily

I've never been the kind of guy who I'm driving past
now this guy home on his lunch break
for no more than a ham sandwich
and the ticking of a kitchen clock who upon checking
the mail and expecting a stack of envelopes
and perhaps a small package has opened instead an escape
for the stench of a hot-boxed lump of dog shit
and who now must spend what little time the afternoon
promises sweating through his button-down fetching
a pair of tattered garden gloves reaching
into that darkness that next dimension of who
and why and while retching on an empty stomach tossing
a few half-baked chunks into weeds that bend
as I drive past but will grow taller because of him.

Breakdown, Bakertown Road

We finished the day's last suicides,
line work, wind sprints from one wall
to the other, and when we stepped from the gym
into winter—near-empty high school lot
sprawled before us like a blank shore—

steam rose from our gleaming necks
like the coiling away of purpose,
and nothing fit my brother's hands anymore,
not the basketball or stack of textbooks

or steering wheel, and I didn't realize
the two years between us were more than days
and hours, and when he drove us home
there was silence like a ball's slow deflation.
I wasn't sure what, beyond the ease of habit,
kept him from letting one of those back-road curves
swallow and thresh our bodies to chaff.

A late-afternoon rain froze into needles,
plunged slantwise. Over the crest of a hill
on a one-lane road, we both saw it
in the wash of high beams, a hatchback dead
and half in a ditch, a woman turned
toward the back seat, her silhouette sharp
in dusk that tumbled across the fields.

What did I know of the aliens inside my brother's chest?
He spoke to the woman and her three children
as though he'd been, in another lifetime,
a soft redness falling, rocking back and forth
from a dogwood to the ground, or an ocean tide
massaging a beach's knotted shoulders.

I'm thinking now if he'd sped by
and hadn't packed them into our back seat,
hadn't laid our jackets across their laps,
hadn't driven them fifteen miles
in the opposite direction, it's likely nothing
would have changed. The next year

we still would have skipped our grandfather's
funeral for a party. That stranded mother
would have done what she had to, waved down
someone else or hiked to the nearest house,
youngest straddling her neck, the others tucked close.

The gym where we dribbled and squeaked our shoes
and dripped our sweat onto hardwood is not haunted
by our forgetting of it. Where we stood that night, the ditch
where we left that car, is now air over mud and weeds.

The only part left is my brother's hands, fuller,
and how he buried them in his pockets, how he walked
the mother and her children to their door,
how he turned away only after the lights switched on.

Watching *The Young & the Restless*

The summer I turned ten, our old brick house needed fixing:
slumped gutters, deck boards warped, screen door slack
like the dog's heavy panting. My dad retired earlier that spring.
Each dawn, he'd disappear from bed, return to the couch
shirtless with paint-splotched shorts and two bananas
just in time for his new ritual: a soap opera.

I'd yawn downstairs, starry-eyed, never asking
the difference between a coping and a hacksaw,
just plop down next to him and watch Jack sip wine
at the ritzy old-boys club, rival Victor blurred in the background.

My dad would finish the first banana by the midpoint,
prop the browning peel like a wig on his bald knee.
I'd pluck it up, drop it into the compost at the next set
of commercials that promised to scrub and flood away
each small impurity men were never meant to see.
He'd unpeel the next only when I'd sat back down, and we'd hope
for a second half with a busted affair or rare fistfight.

By the time school began, we were hooked. He'd pick me up
out front at the three o'clock bell, and I'd ask if he taped
the day's episode. This was how we passed the entire year—
watching Jack and Victor sleep with each woman in town,
brawl over business deals, bicker over manhood;
watching those men turn circles around the true self.

I never saw how, but in that year, while I slept,
he changed our house into something we could sell,
something with its scars hidden, glossed with paint
and mortar. Raised beds sprouting morning glories
and tomatoes in wormy dirt we composted together.

We wouldn't cast long shadows in the same town
or build a dynasty with inherited traits and know-how.
We'd move cross-country and start again with a house
not nearly as broken, and he would still dangle banana peels
and not make me lay shingles, and each day we'd watch
that other set of lives carried out, captured by scandal
and elusive pleasure, and we'd learn a different kind
of inheritance like the slow revolving of the rotting things
we buried each new spring into story.

Heart Attack Grill, Las Vegas, NV

A man ate a burger large as a bear skull,
and now, while I wait to be seated, a nurse
wheels him in a chair up Fremont
and into the neon pulse of downtown Vegas,
past a Surgeon General's warning
painted red on the street-side window.

It was Dr. Jon's Octuple Bypass:
eight beef patties butchered like arteries
from a groin, griddled on scabs of charred batter,
grafted with forty bacon slices
onto the delicious heart, restarted.

Another nurse in a white frock cut tight
at the end of her thighs croons *this way,*
seats me at a candy-red booth,
hands me a menu of brand-name meds
(Prime Angus, 4-ounce shots
of Jack Daniel's, Lucky Strikes,
Just Like Dad! Candy Cigarettes),
and before she turns to make her rounds,
she whispers in my ear
that she'll be taking *extra special care . . .*

And this is how it happens—so instantly,
three words coupled with unbearable need
flood to mind thirty days in the hospital,
my father's chest unzipped under scalpel,
my mother's sexless clutching of his shoulders
as he wrestled nights of apnea and bad trips on Ambien.

And though I know she doesn't, I hope
that by *extra special care* this woman means
she'd have come around each night shift,

strangling sleep, to check his breathing
or wash his purpled inner thigh.

After placing my order, I watch the largest patients
step onto the restaurant's centerpiece, its prep-room scale,
where they hope to weigh more than 350,
their meal paid for per the Grill's insurance policy.

Above their heads, digital numbers flit until they decide
to settle on a clock's hallucinations—
285, 367, 399—the same clock that burned
straight across from my father's post-op bed.

And though I know it's all a show, I can't help but imagine
what he might say if he were here across the table,
tapping the butt ends of his fork and knife,
giddy to bless the coming Bypass and go right back at it,

what he might remember apart from the tapestry
of tubes and wires, desperate shuffles to the bathroom,
setbacks, fluctuating opiates, the heart-shaped pillow
he pulled close to cough; apart from Lipitor, Ativan,
and Diovan and broken tidbits of dream dissolved
into nothing chronological, nothing loyal to memory,
apart from how he could never be left alone—

Only that motherfucking clock! he'd bellow, rattling
the silverware with a downward blow of his fists—
he'd say it shape-shifted hours of pain-killed half-sleep
into the small ticking away of a new life.

And as Dr. Jon hollers out numbers across
the dining room—waiting room, operating room—
to cheers and fist pumps, the traces of my father
vanish without another word, and before I'm ready
a ringing bell pulls whoops of *Kill-It-Dead*

close, and strange fingertips prickle down my back
like trickling water, and the hulking thing,
the beast, is set over my lap, and knowing
exactly all the reasons I shouldn't, I eat.

U.S. History, 11th Grade

Twice a week, our teacher fits the next tape
of the educational video series into the VCR.
          desk lamp switched off
          her eyes beyond the window
The intro montage:
                    she sips a Diet Coke
trumpet-flourish, Washington Crossing the Delaware,
an animated map swelling and coloring west, line crews,

we are told to take notes
mushroom cloud, Reagan directing Mr. Gorbachev
to tear down his wall, a man-in-suit beaming into a phone receiver.

Each episode tells the history of one great structure.
          we are told there will be a test we must pass to move on
Powdered wigs in a jungle, a heaven's worth
of rail laid through desert and swamp, split atoms,
bundles of wire strung coast-to-coast.
          and each question
                    will have one correct answer

It is not the history of gunpowder
                    we are told our legacy—our grade—will outlast us
or rail workers jammed in boxcars or Fat Man's
trial run, its irradiated goat's milk,
          for each question we answer
          by circling the corresponding letter
or the scores of black men lynched from telephone poles.

at the top of each page, we write our names in ink

My Student Named Luke

He could be christened anything,
and often is, but for this young man—
flannel winter coat, dirt-patch jeans,
brown hair greased down straight as razors
—his name frames a walking pastoral.

A farm boy from outside Benton, IL,
without book or pencil or paper. Each class
he arrives late, the door's odd and heavy
clicking sound announcing his entrance
as the doorway out opens like a revelation . . .

We recommence. A lecture on such and such.
Today happens to be The Rhetoric of Greek Argument,
which sounds more impressive than it is.

And Luke, halfway through the slideshow,
considering the crux of an ancient theory,
considering his position in relation to a birth
of human thought, asks the fundamental question,
the pure translation of what they've all come to,
of The Gospel of Core Curriculum Standards:
Is this going to be on the test?

Driving I-24 through Kentucky at night,
I think how easy it would be

Miles and miles of frayed ribbon,
graveyard, shoelace, skinny tie.

Index finger twelve to six,
all it would take
to flatten ditch weeds,
cornstalks, peel the car's body
with a tree trunk.

The night will hack you
from its throat, easy enough.

And face it, the dog at home
would wait curled on the doormat
only so long, and there would be
a spark of relief somewhere deep
inside your lover. The silence
would be tremendous.

Field on field cut with latticed vein,
zipper, cello string, patched quilt.

They would stake a roadside cross,
garland it with wildflowers.
Folks would pass.
Nobody would think to forgive you.

Hiding in the Birds

I must first call hunger *bird tracks in the snow.*
  (Even better—*snowfinch prints in a drift.*)

Next, I must massage the back of my jaw where I've pulled out
  twelve teeth to carve a sleek hollow, but I'll show you instead
  claws digging twelve seeds from the earth.
    (*Bird baths of my cheeks.*)

I must not say how it feels to stand in front of a mirror.

I must paint the birds in their numbered stanzas.
  (All-time metaphor—*each peck the fragile breath of resiliency.*
    Puff-chested, braving a frigid wind.)

I must claim the moon cooed to me about sorrow.
I must stuff the birds with breadcrumbs and cotton and sorrow and
  my father must grow black wings and fly back to the stars.

I must not talk about fashion magazines or my empty bowl of hip
  bones.
I must not tell the story of the junco ramming again and again the
  broken feeder.

I must ask that you listen instead about how snowfinches lug
  muskets wherever they march their winged battalion.

  (*Warriors of my heart's wounded flutter.* Something like that—
  how they wear glorious coats of armor against the flash of
  sunlight on snow.)

Everyone Always Said They Would Fall
in Love All Over Again

Years after their last child leaves home,
the bins, tipped sideways,
wobble in the breeze at their curbs,
each unburdened of garbage,
wanting, perhaps, to roll.

The father, inside, watches his stories.
During commercials aimed at stay-at-home mothers
he stares out the front window
and thinks about kicking their bin along,
how each emptied thing magnets away.

There are details he cannot remember:
their daughter's exact age, the atomic weight
of barium, where he left his loafers.

But his stories, those are familiar enough:
Victor foils, again, Jack's power play;
Sharon cheats; children grow
faster than the days would allow but remain,
always, in the city their parents built.

The mother, outside, feeds
wet cotton and denim to clothespins
even though purple and yellow
spread across the cracked slice of sky
like plum jam and margarine.

The swaying line conducts the symphony
of easy creak and wind chime, and they
don't speak much, but sometimes she says
she wants to keep it all the same,
beds made, two bins out back—though now
they only need one—just in case.

Later, forced inside by the storm,
she offers to make cookies, a single batch,
and he asks for gingerbread.
She nods, though it is not the right season,
and he was the one who always hated ginger.

Concussed

Five Saturdays, in that thunderous bowl
on the river, he was lifted, driven to the turf,
skull-shook. Five times he stumbled off the football field,
dazed, forgetting to raise a finger to the Lord.

We, the college crowd, drunk on whiskey and heat
and wanting it all to hinge on each slant
and post, claimed everything ours.

Now, a few years after his brush with hometown fame,
he and I swing by the liquor store one night for a case
of something cheap and silver. He insists on paying.
Insists we should hang out more. That he loves me.
No homo; like a brother.

The machine declines his card and without a chance
to stop himself he calls the cashier a *cunt*
loud enough for the store to ripple quiet and heavy
like a river gulping a skipped stone.

The cashier is wide-eyed, almost amused,
and a young woman searching bottom-shelf vodka
peers over the aisles to the counter.

He slaps a twenty, scoops the case in one graceful motion
and is out the door before a word can break the silence.

I know he doesn't want to explain himself again,
that all he'd say is *You just saw it for yourself,*
and I can't ask him what's happening
because we were never actually that close of friends.

Once, he said to me on the phone that God
had tested his faith and spirit with the traumas—

and now I close my eyes, see him hawking
across the middle in front of a hundred thousand,
imagine his highlight reel, those moments
of bat-shit elation, and I think how a city of voices
praising his name might coincide with belief.

A few blocks down, we find an empty curb and pop
open a couple. I ask him what I can—
if it was worth it, to be broken so quickly.

Never been asked that, he says,
crumpling the first can in his palm.
But yeah, I wouldn't change a thing.

Austin Kodra lives with his family in Knoxville, TN, where he is training to become a mental health counselor. He received his MFA from Southern Illinois University Carbondale, and his poetry and fiction have been published in *The Adroit Journal, Harpur Palate, Superstition Review, Connotations Press: an Online Artifact, Prime Number Magazine, Valparaiso Fiction Review,* and elsewhere.

CPSIA information can be obtained at www.ICGtesting.com
Printed in the USA
LVOW12s2149080216

474252LV00003B/3/P